I'M A SLAVE
TO FOOD

Shannon Kay McCoy

Consulting Editor: Dr. Paul Tautges

©2014 Shannon Kay McCoy

ISBN
Paper: 978-1-63342-027-4
ePub: 978-1-63342-028-1
Kindle: 978-1-63342-029-8

Shepherd Press
P.O. Box 24
Wapwallopen, PA 18660

www.shepherdpress.com

Designed by **documen**

CONTENTS

INTRODUCTION

I wonder why you have picked up this mini-book. Perhaps it is because the use of the word "slave" in connection with eating habits resonates with you. On the other hand, maybe you have loved ones, friends or coworkers who are battling this issue and you want to help them.

When we hear the word "slave", we think of someone who is helpless under the power of a dominating force or influence. If you are a slave to food, your time and thoughts are devoted to eating it. It seems to have an irresistible power over you, and you give in to it repeatedly. You have lost all hope of ever escaping on your own. You find yourself in a vicious cycle of dieting and overeating. But, if you look around, you know that you are not alone. You can't go through the grocery store checkout line or watch a TV program without being bombarded by the latest diet plan that will revolutionize your life. It seems as though everyone is looking for a solution to stop overeating. Perhaps you have come to the point where you have tried everything and nothing has worked. You find yourself locked behind the prison wall of overeating.

Your food issues are not just about what you are eating, but why you are eating beyond what your body needs. Do you eat merely to satisfy your hunger and nutritional needs? Or do you eat because "it's time" to eat? Do you eat because you are stressed, bored, depressed, anxious, or trying to numb other negative emotions? Or do you eat because you're happy and celebrating an event? Are you using food to meet what you perceive to be your spiritual or emotional needs?

I have written this mini-book for two reasons. First, my interest in this topic is very personal. There have been times in my life when I was a slave to food. You could say that food was my drug of choice. It consumed my life. I tried to use food as a balm for unwanted emotions or as a distraction from undesired responsibilities. Food brought me a false sense of pleasure and satisfaction—but I ended up feeling only confused and betrayed. Today, by God's empowering grace, I am walking victoriously in the truth spoken by Jesus, that "life is more than food" (Luke 12:23) and "man shall not live on bread alone, but on every word that proceeds out of the mouth of God" (Matthew 4:4). I realized that food was not a magic pill to make all my problems go away. I turned to Jesus for real. I surrendered my sinful motives to him. Then, and only then, was I able to experience John 8:32: "and you will know the truth, and the truth will make you free."

Second, I'm concerned about the effectiveness of the Christian church. Excessive overeating, which is called "gluttony" in the Bible, can no longer be considered a subtle, respectable, and silent sin. It is hindering the spiritual growth and effectiveness of many Christians. In the Bible, excessive eating and drinking are often associated with each other. Proverbs 23:21 and Deuteronomy 21:20 put overeating in the same category as drunkenness. Elyse Fitzpatrick says, "Think about it as the difference between having a glass of wine with dinner and getting drunk. Gluttony is similar to getting drunk on food."[1] If alcoholics were attending your church, would you not have the compassion to reach out to them and help them? The same thing goes for church members who are in bondage to overeating.

This little book isn't the latest diet plan for losing weight. It is a compass to point you in the direction of getting to the heart of your overeating and to lead you to the only way of escape, which is through Jesus Christ. Only Jesus can truly bring you out of slavery and into true freedom.

In order for this book to help you, you must be a true believer in Jesus Christ. If you are unsure of your standing with God, I urge you to take this moment to be certain that Jesus is the Savior and Lord of your life. Let's look at what the Bible tells us about ourselves:

We Are Born Sinners and Separated from God

The book of Genesis tells us the origin of man. As God's creation, Adam and Eve were perfect—without sin—until they disobeyed God and ate the forbidden fruit (Genesis 3:6). Their disobedience has caused everyone to be born into sin, to live in a fallen world, and ultimately to face the deserved punishment of death and hell.

> Therefore, just as through one man sin entered into the world, and death through sin, and so death spread to all men, because all sinned ...
>
> (Romans 5:12)

But God, in his great wisdom, already had a plan in place to reverse the curse of sin.

God Has a Plan to Reconcile Sinners to Himself

Since God hates sin, we can't have fellowship with him. The only way to restore our relationship with God is to have the penalty of our sin, which is death, paid in full. Jesus is the only one qualified to pay the penalty of death because of his sinless life. Therefore, God sent Jesus to die on the cross, taking God's punishment for us so that we could be set free from all sin. God showed that the sin-debt had been paid by raising Jesus from the dead and seating him at his right hand in heaven.

> For Christ also died for sins once for all,
> the just for the unjust, so that He might
> bring us to God, having been put to death
> in the flesh, but made alive in the spirit.
>
> (1 Peter 3:18)

God Offers Us a Free Gift

Because of Jesus' death and resurrection, God offers us forgiveness of our sins. The gift is that we can have our sins forgiven and be at peace with God through Jesus Christ.

> Therefore, having been justified by faith,
> we have peace with God through our Lord
> Jesus Christ.
>
> *(Romans 5:1)*

You Must Receive this Gift by Faith

This free gift is yours

> if you confess with your mouth Jesus as
> Lord, and believe in your heart that God
> raised Him from the dead ...; for with
> the heart a person believes, resulting in
> righteousness, and with the mouth he
> confesses, resulting in salvation.
>
> *(Romans 10:9–10)*

If you agree with God that you are a sinner, and if you want to be reconciled to him, cry out to him for mercy. Believe what Jesus did for you on the cross and that he rose again on your behalf, and ask God to forgive your sins and to put you in a right standing with him. If you do this, you will be saved from the penalty and power of sin.

1

Is Food Your Master?

Victoria described her relationship with food as a love affair. It began early in her life. As a child, she realized that the only thing she could control in her life was eating. Food was her friend, her secret pal and her lover. She would plan special times to be with her favorite foods. At first, it was fun and exciting; it gave her great pleasure. She didn't know that one day she would weigh 290 pounds. Victoria felt estranged from God. She couldn't even pray that he would help her. She didn't even want to know how much money she threw away on this false dream of fulfillment. She tried every diet under the sun, believing each time that she'd achieve lasting victory. Sadly, Victoria discovered that victory never lasted beyond three weeks. She found some physical success with a few diet plans, but eventually she'd quit and gain even more weight. She thought her weight was the problem. All she needed was to find the plan that worked for her, and then she would be happy.

Victoria had asked God so many times to just

fix her and make her stop eating so much that she felt that God wasn't listening or didn't care. Every time she looked at herself in the mirror or had to attend a formal event or a class reunion, she would beg, plead, and bargain with God to take away the excess weight. She was angry with God. She just wanted him to get her out of her "fat suit." She blamed God, her parents, her husband, her kids, her boss, and even food itself. Though she treated food as her lover, it became her betrayer. She felt enslaved by it. It seemed as though it called her and tempted her to the point that she'd give in every time. She was out of control and thought about food most of the day, every day. While she was finishing one meal, she was already thinking about the next. She felt that she was a slave to food.

The Slave–Master Relationship

Like Victoria, you may describe yourself as a slave to food. A slave is a person held in servitude or bondage, with a resulting loss of freedom. A slave is completely subservient to a master. The master has ownership, authority, power, and control over the life of a slave.

Is food really your master? If so, food has

ownership of you. It has exclusive rights over your life. It is your authority. It influences or commands your thoughts and behavior. It has supreme power over you. It forces you to obey its commands. You are forever at its disposal. It has taken away your freedom of choice. Food is heartless and puts insurmountable pressure on you, even to the point of death.

As a slave, you recognize your desperate condition. Naturally, you want to be free from food's tyranny. You try to find ways to escape from your difficult situation. You try many ways of escape, but to no avail. You begin to hate food for its abuse of you.

What is the answer to your problem? We must start with the truth. Food cannot be your master because it is a substance created by God to provide nutritional support for the body in order to produce energy, stimulate growth, and maintain life. In actuality, you are trying to be the master over food. You love the taste and the chemical effect it has on your body. However, you have taken what God intended for good and perverted it, turning it into something it is not. Your desire is to have food fulfill a need in you that only God can fill. Weight gain and other health related ailments shine the spotlight on your excessive eating habits;

therefore, you hate food because it exposes you. Nevertheless, you also love it, because it gives you pleasure. Perhaps it is this love–hate relationship with food that caused you to pick up this book in the first place.

The Bible presents overeating as sin, so we must now examine why it does so.

2

Exposing the Sin of Overeating

You need to know the foundational truths about overeating before you can live in the freedom that is awaiting you. Let's look at it from God's perspective.

Overeating Is a Sin

God declares overeating to be a sin:

> For the heavy drinker and the glutton will come to poverty ...
>
> (Proverbs 23:21)

There are several definitions of sin in the Bible:

» "The devising of folly is sin" (Proverbs 24:9).

» "Whatever is not from faith is sin" (Romans 14:23).

» "Therefore, to one who knows the right thing to do and does not do it, to him it is sin" (James 4:17).

» "All unrighteousness is sin" (1 John 5:17).

» "Sin is lawlessness" (1 John 3:4).

These descriptions view sin as the act of your will. Sin is choosing to act in opposition to God's Word. Perhaps you don't believe that overeating is a sin. Many of us have been brainwashed by magazine articles, television talk shows, and reality shows that tell us that food is the problem: you are simply eating the wrong things in the wrong way. Often even the Christian perspective views overeating as a diet problem rather than a sin problem. On the other hand, you may know that overeating is a sin, but it does not seem serious because it is often treated as one of those "little sins" that are acceptable in the church. You don't hear sermons or read books on the sin of overeating. Your focus is more on getting treatment for your problem of overeating than facing up to your personal responsibility of repentance and obedience.

According to the above descriptions of sin, overeating is of folly, not of faith. It is failing to do the right thing. It is unrighteousness and lawlessness. The following is a testimony from someone who struggled with overeating:

*My eating was out of control. I ate solely
to satisfy whatever craving I was having
at the time. As a result, my health was
suffering and I was not honoring God with
my life and body He had given me. I was
for the first time confronted with the fact
that the way that I was eating was sinful. I
knew that my eating was "not good," but I
never considered that my eating was sin.*[2]

Overeating Dominates Your Life

Overeating is a life-dominating sin, and it has a
strong influence over your life. It affects your mind,
your body, your spirit, your heart, your emotions,
your relationships, and even your finances. The
sin of overeating is practiced repeatedly so that
it becomes a habitual lifestyle and almost second
nature, a continuous action that controls your life.

When our lives reflect one particular
characteristic, we are known by that characteristic.
For example, a habitual drinker is a drunkard,
a habitual teller of lies is a liar—and a habitual
overeater is a glutton.

Let's look at a few characteristics of the life-
dominating sin of overeating.

YOU HAVE REPEATEDLY TRIED TO STOP

You've tried every diet known to man, but failed to stop habitually overeating. The root of your problem is that you are not taking this sin seriously. Overeating is not some frivolous behavior.

YOU BLAME OTHERS OR CIRCUMSTANCES FOR YOUR FAILURE TO STOP

The world may teach you to blame your mother for your sinful eating habits because, when you were a child, she forced you to "clean your plate" at every meal. You may blame it on your genetic makeup: you see that every woman in your family is overweight; therefore, it is beyond your control. You may blame your problem on the diet plan. You say, "It did not work for me. It is too strict." You may even blame your sin on God because he will not change your circumstances, your cravings, and so on. You completely disregard what the apostle Paul says in Romans 14:12:

> So then each one of us will give an
> account of himself to God.

You must know that if you are a Christian, God is your authority and overseer. You will one day have to give an account for your actions to God.

YOU DENY THAT OVEREATING IS A SIN

You believe what the world tells you about your overeating problem. You believe that your problem is really low self-esteem, or that you actually have a disease. You refuse to accept that your actions are sinful and do not glorify God. You call it a weakness instead of a sin. You disregard Scripture's statement about sin:

> If we say that we have no sin, we are
> deceiving ourselves and the truth is not
> in us.
>
> (1 John 1:8)

If you don't believe the truth of God's Word, there isn't any hope for you. In 1 John 1:9, you are instructed to confess your sins. You must confess that your overeating is a sin against God.

YOU CONVINCE YOURSELF THAT YOU ARE NOT ENSLAVED TO OVEREATING AND "CAN STOP AT ANY TIME"

You must admit that you are in bondage to the sin of overeating. Jesus teaches,

> Everyone who commits sin is the slave
> of sin.
>
> (John 8:34)

You believe that you are in control of your eating habits every time you start a new diet plan or workout program. You are deceived into believing that this plan will deliver you. A life-dominating sin requires the work of the Holy Spirit in order for it to be put to death in the believer. You cannot defeat this sin in your own strength. Your hope lies in knowing the truth. You must stop believing the lies your sin promises you, and instead believe God's truth.

ANY PLEASURE FROM OVEREATING IS SHORT-LIVED, WHILE THE HARM IS CONSIDERABLE AND LONG-TERM

You feel as though you have no control over your cravings. You give in to the temptation to eat repeatedly. You see your body weight increasing and feel your clothes tightening. You get depressed because you don't like the way you look. Your blood pressure is getting dangerously high, and your knees hurt when you try to climb the stairs to your apartment. Nevertheless, you find yourself stuffing your face again with massive amounts of food and not receiving the relief you are seeking. You feel overstuffed, uncomfortable, and numb, instead of content and satisfied.

YOU OVEREAT WHEN NO ONE IS WATCHING

When overeating controls you, you will seek to hide your outward behavior by doing it in secret. You will go through a fast-food restaurant drive-through and order two value size combos. By the time you pull into your driveway, all evidence of gluttonous behavior is gone. You quickly dispose of the trash and the aroma from your car before you greet your family. As your weight increases because of eating too much, you try to hide your body by wearing oversized clothes. Hiding your sin will only lead you into deeper bondage. You must realize that there is power in confession. James 5:16 states,

> Therefore, confess your sins to one
> another, and pray for one another so that
> you may be healed. The effective prayer of
> a righteous man can accomplish much.

When you confess your sin to another believer, that believer is obligated to pray for you, and spiritual healing takes place.

YOU KNOW THAT OVEREATING OBSCURES THE TESTIMONY OF JESUS CHRIST IN YOUR LIFE AND IS A STUMBLING BLOCK TO OTHERS

To commit sin and know that it is damaging the

testimony of Jesus Christ can lead you more deeply into slavery. You must know that your sinful actions are affecting everyone around you: your husband, children, coworkers, unsaved relatives, and friends. You cannot admonish and encourage others in their walk with Christ when you are purposefully committing sin in their presence. They see your helpless struggle with overeating and may deny the power of Christ in their own lives.

YOU KNOW THAT GOD'S WORD TELLS YOU TO STOP SINNING, AND THAT GOD CAN RELEASE YOU FROM THIS BONDAGE

Pride and rebellion are at the heart of your problem. Perhaps you have been a Christian for a long time and you know that God is not pleased with your gluttonous behavior. But you continue to ignore God's command to glorify him when you eat (1 Corinthians 10:31). You revel in your indulgence. You are self-reliant and proud of it. You refuse to trust in God's faithfulness and accept his way of escape (1 Corinthians 10:13). You must know that God's ways are indeed sufficient.

YOU REALIZE THAT YOUR DEEDS (THOUGHTS, WORDS, ACTIONS) DO NOT CONFORM TO THE CHARACTER OF CHRIST

Your conscience accuses you of your sin. Your

behavior doesn't conform to the character of Christ. Without telling a bold-faced lie, you cannot say that your gluttonous behavior is Christlike. You know in your heart that your behavior is not pleasing to the Lord. You know that your desire is to please yourself. To justify your sinful indulgence you may even bring up the passage in Matthew 11:19 where Jesus was accused of being a glutton: "The Son of Man came eating and drinking, and they say, 'Behold, a gluttonous man and a drunkard, a friend of tax collectors and sinners!'" This passage, however, does not show that Jesus was a glutton, but that the people were fickle in their understanding of the truth. Likewise are you, if you refuse to admit that your gluttonous behavior does not comply with the character of Jesus Christ.

Overeating Is a Spiritual Problem

Some overeaters describe themselves as having an addiction to food. The world may use this terminology to describe the behavior of someone who is controlled by a substance. The Merriam-Webster dictionary defines addiction in this way: "To devote or surrender (oneself) to something habitually or obsessively."[4] In the world of psychology, gluttony or overeating is officially recognized as an addiction. Although the word *addiction* is not found in the Bible, there are passages that describe what is meant by addiction.

> Jesus answered them, "Truly, truly, I say to you, everyone who commits sin is the slave of sin."
>
> (John 8:34)

> [B]y what a man is overcome, by this he is enslaved.
>
> (2 Peter 2:19b)

> The evil deeds of the wicked ensare them; the cords of their sins hold them fast.
>
> (Proverbs 5:22)

The danger in labeling overeating an addiction is that it undermines the personal conviction of sin. If sin is not the problem then you will look for solutions from a system of theories, not in the person of Jesus Christ. The biblical perspective of addiction however, offers hope to those who feel helplessly trapped in their habit of overeating.

Overeating Is Idolatry

The biblical term for "addiction" is "idolatry." The sin of overeating is idolatry. Idolatry is worship and devotion to creation rather than worship and devotion to the Creator God. You worship your stomach and appetites by indulging in food. You desire the created food more than your Creator. The problem is not necessarily the food you consume; it is the worship of your heart. The phrase "idols in their hearts" was first mentioned in Ezekiel 14:3–6:

> Son of man, these men have set up their
> idols in their hearts and have put right
> before their faces the stumbling block of
> their iniquity. Should I be consulted by
> them at all? Therefore speak to them and
> tell them, "Thus says the Lord GOD, 'Any
> man of the house of Israel who sets up his
> idols in his heart, puts right before his face
> the stumbling block of his iniquity, and
> then comes to the prophet, I the LORD
> will be brought to give him an answer in
> the matter in view of the multitude of his
> idols, in order to lay hold of the hearts of
> the house of Israel who are estranged from

*Me through all their idols."' Therefore say
to the house of Israel, "Thus says the Lord
GOD, 'Repent and turn away from your
idols and turn your faces away from all
your abominations."'*

In this passage, the elders of Israel came to
Ezekiel, the prophet, for godly advice. God,
knowing their hearts, revealed to Ezekiel that
the men worshipped other gods and put wicked
obstacles "before their faces." These hypocritical
elders were courting the true God while all along
having other lovers or idols in their hearts. Old
Testament commentators Keil and Delitzsch say
that idol worship means "to allow anything to
come into the mind, to permit it to rise up in the
heart, to be mentally busy therewith."[5] God, in his
sovereignty, did not give them what they desired,
but instead gave them what they needed. He
exposed their sin and called them to repentance.

How does this passage apply to you? First, you
have set up an idol in your heart. You have made
food a god that you bow down to and worship.
Second, you have put before your face the
stumbling block of your iniquity. You continue
to give yourself access to food for the purpose
of indulgence. Then you come to God asking for

the desires of your heart. God is not obligated to answer your prayers when you refuse to trust in his sovereignty. When you harbor idolatry in your heart, God deals with the idolatry first. You may think he doesn't hear your prayers because you ignore his promptings to deal with the idol in your heart. Before you can be set free, however, you must acknowledge your idol, denounce it, repent, and give your heart and devotion to him. Your greatest hope is in turning from your false gods and surrendering your life to Jesus, who is able to forgive your sins and free you from the sin of overeating.

3

Sin Shall Not Be Master Over You

You may be feeling helpless right now. You have accepted the reality that overeating is a sin. You may be confused about what you are discovering about yourself. A part of you may want to surrender your overeating to God. On the other hand, you really don't want to give it up. You find yourself in a tug-of-war. To be free from the sin of overeating, you must understand what it means to be dead to sin and alive to God.

The Bible explains this in Romans 6. How does that chapter apply to your struggle? The apostle Paul teaches five truths about Christians:

You Have Died to Sin (vv. 1–2)

Jesus died in your place (Romans 5:6–8), and you are dead to sin. In Romans 6:2, the apostle Paul asks a rhetorical question: "How shall we who died to sin still live in it?" He is declaring the impossibility of a Christian living in sin.

If you are in Christ, it is now against your new nature to live habitually in sin.

You Have Been Spiritually Baptized and Have Union with Jesus Christ (vv. 3–10)

You are spiritually immersed into the person of Jesus Christ. You are also identified with him in his resurrection. Through his death and resurrection, you are regenerated. You no longer identify with the sin life, but now identify with the resurrected life of Jesus Christ. Your old self died with Christ and, as the apostle declares, you now live the life of Christ.

> I have been crucified with Christ; and it
> is no longer I who live, but Christ lives in
> me; and the life which I now live in the
> flesh I live by faith in the Son of God, who
> loved me, and gave Himself up for me.
> (Galatians 2:20)

Jesus' death on the cross not only paid the penalty for sin, but it also broke the power of indwelling sin in your life. The presence and control of your old unregenerate self have no power over you. The sin of overeating does not have power over you. If you are dead to the sin of overeating, you are free not to overeat. Nothing forces you to overeat—despite your excuses.

At this point, you might be thinking, "I may be free not to overeat, but I can't stop doing it." This is a crucial point in your journey to victory. Your doubt is coming from your sinful thoughts, which are lies. You have a slave mentality, which causes you to think and act as a slave. You believe that food is your master and that you will never be free from its grip. You are a prisoner of your mind; you can't conceive what it means to be free. Freedom from the sin of overeating is what Romans 6 is teaching you. Jesus breaks the burdensome yoke of the slave mentality.

You Have Been Made Alive to God (vv. 11–13)

Romans 6:11 states,

> *Even so consider yourselves to be dead to sin, but alive to God in Christ Jesus.*

If you are dead to sin, you are free to live for God. Paul urges you to consider, or believe by faith, what God has revealed to be true. Being alive to God is living in his truth and his presence.

As an overeater, you live in your own truth. You live for yourself, believing that you need or deserve to indulge in food to receive satisfaction. Blinded by the deception of overeating, you are not aware of or sensitive to the presence of God.

You may ask, "How can an overeater become alive to God and be more aware of his presence?" Paul gives us four significant instructions:

"DO NOT LET SIN REIGN IN YOUR MORTAL BODY SO THAT YOU OBEY ITS LUSTS" (v. 12)

You are commanded not to allow the sin of overeating to take control of your body, because you will submit to its lusts. This is a command, not a suggestion. Since you are dead to sin and alive to God, sin is no longer your master. You are no longer helpless. You must make the decision to say "no" to the sin of overeating and "yes" to God.

In Genesis 4, we find the sad story of Cain, the firstborn child of Adam and Eve. He had a brother named Abel, whom he hated. Cain had evil in his heart toward Abel because Abel was devoted to God and lived a righteous life. Cain was a reprobate and resented Abel.

At the time of worship, Abel's offering was acceptable to God and Cain's was unacceptable. Cain got angry and killed Abel. God confronted

Cain, and Genesis 4:6–7 states,

> Then the LORD said to Cain, "Why are you
> angry? And why has your countenance
> fallen? If you do well, will not your
> countenance be lifted up? And if you do not
> do well, sin is crouching at the door; and its
> desire is for you, but you must master it."

God mercifully gave Cain a choice. He could do what was right: acknowledge his sin, his self-righteousness, and the idols in his heart, repent, and then obey what God told him to do. If he obeyed God, joy would manifest itself in his countenance. If he disobeyed, sin would dominate his life.

Unremorseful, Cain made the wrong choice and reaped the consequences. The command for you is this: "Stop allowing overeating to reign in your body so that you give in to its cravings over and over again." You can choose to let overeating master you, or you can master overeating by obeying God's commands.

"DO NOT GO ON PRESENTING THE MEMBERS OF YOUR BODY TO SIN AS INSTRUMENTS OF UNRIGHTEOUSNESS" (v. 13)

Paul is urging you to keep watch over the members— the parts—of your body: what your eyes look at, your ears listen to, your mind thinks about, your hands do, and where your feet carry you. This is very practical. You must make the effort to stay away from temptation as much as possible. Do not look at commercials and media ads showing tempting foods. Do not listen to or engage in conversations about indulging in foods. Do not let your mind fantasize about tempting foods. Do not allow yourself to fondle tempting foods. Do not allow yourself to hang out where there will be tempting foods. If you fail to make these choices based on the power of Jesus Christ, you will be living an unrighteous life.

"Present Yourselves to God as Those Alive from the Dead" (v. 13)

Your union with Jesus made you alive from the dead. As an overeater, you are like a dead person. You are lifeless and without joy. Your sin leads only to death. However, you have been given new life in Christ and share in his resurrection. Now, you must make the decision to live for God once and for all. Let your eating habits glorify God.

"Present ... Your Members as Instruments of Righteousness to God" (v. 13)

Let your eyes, ears, mouth, mind, hands, and feet glorify God. You must make every effort to let your eyes look for the healthy foods that will nourish, sustain, and heal your body. Let your ears listen to wisdom from God concerning your eating habits. Let your mouth speak words that will edify others to eat to the glory of God. Let your mind be filled with thoughts that are true, honorable, right, pure, lovely, of good repute, excellent, and worthy of praise (Philippians 4:8) when it comes to eating right, losing weight, and exercising. Let your hands prepare foods that are good for you, your family, and your friends. Let your feet take you to places where you can serve food to those in need.

You Have Been Freed from the Dominion of Sin (vv. 14–20)

Jesus left heaven and came down to earth to die on the cross for our sins so that sin's power over us would be broken. Sin has been dethroned, and now Jesus reigns in the hearts of all believers. Romans 6:14 states,

> For sin shall not be master over you, for you are not under law but under grace.

The Old Testament law was meant to reveal our inability to live a righteous life, but God's grace enables us to live such a life in the power of Jesus Christ. As an overeater, you have been living under the law. You have tried everything and used all your physical energy to try to stop overeating, but to no avail. You can't be set free without Christ. It is only by faith in the grace of Jesus Christ that you will be set free from the sin of overeating.

You Have Been Freed from Sin which Leads to Death, and Been Enslaved to God for Everlasting Life (vv. 21–23)

In order to walk in freedom, you must walk by faith in the fact that you are no longer a slave to the sin of overeating. You were walking in a pathway that leads to death. In Christ, you are free from sin and free to serve God in your eating habits. Your part is to put your faith in Jesus and obey what he says about your eating habits. Trust that he will enable you to walk in total victory.

The Evil Trinity

You must be aware and alert to the evil trinity in the Christian's life. You have three forces against you in your battle with overeating: the enticements

of the world (1 John 2:16), the stubbornness of the
flesh (Romans 8:7–8), and the craftiness of the
devil (John 8:44). You are constantly attacked in
all three spheres.

THE WORLD

The world is the domain in which sin reigns and is
in rebellion against God. It alienates people from
God and keeps them in bondage to sin. It plays a
powerful role in the development and destruction
of the overeater. It is oriented toward sin, and its
agenda is to pull you into all sorts of sin, especially
the sin of overeating. In 1 John 2:15, the apostle
John says,

> Do not love the world nor the things in
> the world. If anyone loves the world, the
> love of the Father is not in him.

The sin of overeating represents love for the
world. It is the world's mission to destroy your
love for God by appealing to your inner cravings
and desires. It steals your love away from the
Father. You cannot love the world and God at the
same time.

The world attacks you in three significant areas
of your heart. First John 2:16 states,

> *For all that is in the world, the lust of*
> *the flesh and the lust of the eyes and*
> *the boastful pride of life, is not from the*
> *Father, but is from the world.*

Lust of the Flesh

The word "flesh" refers to the sin nature that is in opposition to God. It lusts after those things that contradict God's standards. It makes a god out of its appetites. As an overeater, you seek comfort. You could choose God's way or the world's way. The world appeals to your natural desires and tempts you to satisfy them in unbiblical ways. In stressful times, you run to your favorite food instead of to God, who is the "God of all comfort" (2 Corinthians 1:3).

Lust of the Eyes

You lust with your eyes when you covet a certain body image. The world tells you how you should look in order to be acceptable. Through magazines such as *Elle* and *Men's Health*, and TV shows such as *Lost* and *America's Next Top Model*, the world dictates how our bodies are to look in terms of height, weight, and shape. You try many different diets and exercise programs to get your body to meet the world's standards, and, when you fail, you run to food to drown your sorrows. You feel ashamed, self-conscious, and anxious about your body. This lust drives the overeater into a cycle of dieting and excessive eating.

Boastful Pride of Life

The "pride of life" means making a god out of control and power. The world tells you that you can look like a supermodel if you will embrace its philosophies. You listen to the world's wisdom and begin to boost your self-esteem. You take part in the new and expensive weight-loss phenomenon. When you begin to lose weight, you receive praise and applause from your family and friends. You take pride in having the willpower to stop overeating and you condemn others who don't.

THE FLESH

The second enemy represents the sin nature, or the old nature where sin dwells. Our sinful nature will use the body as an instrument for evil. It uses the body to draw us away from God and everything righteous. The sin nature can do nothing to please God.

As you yield to your sin nature it will use your body to get power over you to perform evil acts, such as overeating. It uses your desires, appetites, and senses to express itself. As explained earlier, Romans 6 teaches that the sinful nature lost complete control over you when Jesus saved you. If you are a Christian, you are dead to sin and alive to God. Nevertheless, the sinful nature will keep trying to dominate you. You are not to let the sin of overeating reign over you. You must stop giving your allegiance to the gods of comfort, pride and rebellion, and control and power. The flesh tempts you to bow down to these gods to satisfy your cravings, desires, and perceived needs. You have to bring all the natural functions of your body under the Lordship of Christ so that God's nature will be manifested in your body.

The Devil

The third enemy is a fallen angel and the archenemy of God. His fall from heaven ushered in the spiritual warfare that Christians experience every day. Second Corinthians 10:3–4 proclaims,

> For though we walk in the flesh, we
> do not war according to the flesh, for
> the weapons of our warfare are not of
> the flesh, but divinely powerful for the
> destruction of fortresses.

The devil is the god of this world and his primary target is Jesus Christ. The devil, also called Satan, was defeated when Jesus died on the cross, rose from the dead and ascended into heaven. All who put their faith in Jesus Christ are saved from the devil's power and become his enemy.

Anytime sin is involved in your life, a spiritual war has been declared. The devil's purpose is to destroy everything God created for his glory. Satan's aim is to cast doubt, to devalue, to distort, to deny, to denounce, and to distrust God, his character and his Word.

Satan's desire is to imprison you for life, rendering you ineffective in the Kingdom of God. He deceives you into believing that overeating will bring you happiness and fulfillment. Then, he accuses and condemns you while you are trapped in the sin of overeating. You are responsible for your overeating; nevertheless, satanic influences contribute to and intensify your sinful tendency to overeat. The goal of Satan is to steal, kill, and destroy those who believe in Jesus Christ (John 10:10).

4
Walking in Freedom

In Chapter 1, we met Victoria, who struggles with overeating. Now, she acknowledges that overeating is a sin. She understands that the actual food she eats is not her master. She realizes that, if she is truly a believer in Christ, she is united with Christ in his death and resurrection. Therefore, Victoria considers herself dead to sin and alive to God. She is no longer a slave to sin and unrighteousness, but a voluntary slave to Jesus Christ and righteousness. She rejoices in this wonderful knowledge. However, the next day, she finds herself reverting to her old sinful eating habits. She wonders, "What happened?"

In Luke 11:24–26, Jesus tells a story that illustrates what happens when we try to overcome sinful living without replacing it with righteous living. A demon that has possessed a man is cast out of him. The evil demon travels through dry, desert places, seeking a place to rest. He cannot find a resting place, so he decides to return to the body of the man in whom he previously lived. He arrives to find his old dwelling place swept clean and put in order. The evil spirit then decides to find seven of his most wicked friends so they can live there together. The man's life therefore ends up being worse than it was at first. The demon-possessed man and his exorcist have failed to realize that the power of Jesus Christ is necessary for a complete and final exorcism. Instead, they have relied on their own strength and false religion.

In our attempts to stop overeating, first we ask God to take away the desire to overeat. Then, we determine not to overeat by going on a diet or fasting. By day three, we find ourselves overpowered by the temptation to overeat. We brush ourselves off and determine to try again on Monday. Before the week or day is complete, though, we find ourselves overeating again. Try as we might, we just can't stop overeating.

Renewing the Mind

How, then, are we to experience freedom in Christ? Just having the knowledge that we are dead to sin and alive to God is not enough to experience freedom from sin. Therefore, we focus on the sin. We are determined not to overeat. All our mental energy goes into counting calories, grams of carbohydrates, fats, and protein, portion sizes, cutting out bread, rice, and pasta, red meat or pork—and the list goes on. Our resolve not to overeat only reinforces the sinful eating pattern.

The battlefield is the mind, the central part of our intellect, our beliefs, and understanding, as well as of our emotions, motives, and actions. Sinful behavior begins with our thoughts. Mark 7:21 says,

> For from within, out of the heart of men,
> proceed the evil thoughts.

Life circumstances, such as a difficult boss or a failed marriage, are not the cause of our overeating. They bring out what is already in our hearts, such as anger, sadness, or jealousy. We use these emotions as an excuse to overeat. Then we try to correct the problem by following a weight-loss plan such as WeightWatchers or the Atkins Diet. Once the diet is complete, we start overeating again. Our sinful thoughts must be replaced with the truths of God's plan in order to stop overeating. Ephesians 4:22–24 states,

> In reference to your former manner of life

> ... lay aside the old self, which is being
> corrupted in accordance with the lusts
> of deceit, and ... be renewed in the spirit
> of your mind, and put on the new self,
> which in the likeness of God has been
> created in righteousness and holiness of
> the truth.

This passage gives us the steps to overcoming a sinful habit. Some have referred to this process as the principle of replacement. First, the old self must be put away. This step began at the point of our salvation. The second step is the most overlooked: we are to be renewed in the spirit of our minds. This is the transforming process of having our minds of worldliness changed into the mind of Christ (1 Corinthians 2:16). Our union with Christ grants us the moral and spiritual capability to overcome sinful habits that a mind apart from Christ could never accomplish. The third step is to put on the new self. This step also started at the point of salvation. The "new self" refers to the saved person now dominated by the nature of Jesus Christ. Second Corinthians 5:17 tells us,

> Therefore if anyone is in Christ, he is a
> new creature; the old things passed away;
> behold, new things have come.

The renewing of our minds is the ongoing process of bringing into our minds the reality of what was accomplished by God at the point of salvation (Romans 12:2). It is possible, while being free in Christ, to revert to old sinful habits. Consequently, even though we are liberated, we must grow into this newness of life (Romans 6:4). This is accomplished through the power of the indwelling Holy Spirit when we yield to him (Galatians 5:25). The Holy Spirit enables this transformation by controlling our thinking as we study and meditate on God's Word, producing his own fruit (Galatians 5:22-23). The renewed mind is a mind saturated with and controlled by the whole counsel of the Word of God.

God's Word instructs us in how to combat the dominating influences of the world, the flesh, and the devil. These forces are with us daily. We live in the world, the flesh resides in us, and the devil lurks nearby to find whom he can devour.

Overcoming the World by Faith

We overcome the world by faith in Jesus Christ. The apostle John says in 1 John 5:4-5,

> For whatever is born of God overcomes

> *the world; and this is the victory that has*
> *overcome the world—our faith. Who is*
> *the one who overcomes the world, but he*
> *who believes that Jesus is the Son of God?*

Your hope of freedom lies in the power of Jesus Christ. Jesus warns his disciples that trouble and tribulation await them in the world (John 16:33). However, their hope of overcoming the world is in him. His death and resurrection defeated the whole world system; therefore, you can have full confidence that Jesus will enable you to stop overeating.

Faith in Jesus Christ opposes the wisdom of the world. Instead of seeking the world's solution for the problem of overeating, start seeking God's counsel. Your confident assurance in Jesus supernaturally turns your heart away from the world and back to him. John warns us in 1 John 2:15,

> *Do not love the world nor the things in*
> *the world. If anyone loves the world, the*
> *love of the Father is not in him.*

The sin of overeating steals your love for God, but trust in Jesus increases your love for him.

To love God more than food is to obey him. You disobey God when you fear the displeasure of the world more than the displeasure of God. You fear obesity, bad health, and shame, rather than the chastisement of God and grieving his Spirit. Faith in Jesus gives you the capacity to discern the world's lies and deception. Sinful eating makes you an enemy of God, because you are friends with the world. The Bible says,

> Friendship with the world is hostility toward God.
>
> (James 4:4)

We live in a world that deifies humanity, and wants to remove all forms of suffering and hard work. We embrace that philosophy because we don't want to suffer any pain and we want to feel good about ourselves. However, to accept this philosophy makes you God's enemy.

Overcoming the Flesh by Walking in the Spirit

We learned in Chapter 3 that we are in a battle with our sin nature, which is the flesh. The Holy Spirit controls our new nature. He is the key to victorious Christian living. We received the Holy Spirit when we were saved. He is the dominating force in our lives. These two natures are at war with each other because they have different goals (Romans 8:5–6). The flesh has desires that are evil, but the new nature has desires that are holy. Galatians 5:16–17 says,

> But I say, walk by the Spirit, and you
> will not carry out the desire of the flesh.
> For the flesh sets its desire against the
> Spirit, and the Spirit against the flesh; for
> these are in opposition to one another,
> so that you may not do the things that
> you please.

God commands us to walk by the Spirit so that we won't produce the deeds of the flesh. Walking by the Spirit of God will keep you from falling into the sin of overeating. This is a daily battle. You are not to depend on your own strength, but on the power of the indwelling Holy Spirit. How, then, are we to walk by the Spirit?

YIELD TO THE HOLY SPIRIT
The Holy Spirit does not operate automatically in our hearts, that is, without our obedient

cooperation. We must surrender our wills to him. This may sound simple, but it is difficult to implement. Yielding to the Holy Spirit requires the agonizing mental and painful work of exposing the idols in our hearts. Our flesh screams in rebellion, and we run to food. However, the moment you surrender your will and submit to the Holy Spirit, he blocks the evil cravings of the flesh, enabling you to say "no" to overeating.

Do Not Hinder the Work of the Holy Spirit

One way we hinder the work of the Spirit is through legalistic systems of sanctification. These systems focus only on outward behavioral change to the exclusion of the inner issues of the heart. This type of outward focus is usually found in the form of strict conformity to rules and regulations outside of God's Word and His grace. In a desperate attempt to get your overeating under control, you may use your time, energy, and resources to commit yourself to a strict and specific diet plan. In doing so, you submit to someone else's law in search of freedom from the sin of overeating. The more law-based sanctification you apply to your life, the more you will hinder the work of the Holy Spirit and become a spiritual hypocrite. God's way is not a temporary weight-loss plan, but a long-term, lifestyle change toward eating to His glory. Yielding to the Holy Spirit allows him to enable you to stop overeating, so that God is glorified.

LIVE A SPIRIT-FILLED LIFE

God commands us to be filled with the Spirit. Ephesians 5:18 says,

> And do not get drunk with wine, for that
> is dissipation, but be filled with the Spirit.

Drunkenness is feeding the flesh, which produces sinful deeds and negative consequences. The Spirit-filled life includes a continual feeding on Jesus Christ and his Word. It calls for a deliberate and active life (compare Proverbs 23:21). Being filled with the Spirit starves the flesh. If you cultivate the flesh, you put yourself in a position of temptation. Overeating—gluttony—is like getting drunk, and it is the antithesis of being filled with the Spirit. It is wasteful indulgence with food.

Living the Spirit-filled life involves letting the Word of Christ richly indwell you (Colossians 3:16). When you saturate your soul with the truths found in God's Word, the Holy Spirit has the ammunition to kill all evil desires and to work God's will in your life. The Spirit-filled life is characterized by

speaking to one another in psalms and
hymns and spiritual songs, singing and
making melody with your heart to the
Lord; always giving thanks for all things
in the name of our Lord Jesus Christ to
God, even the Father; and [being] subject
to one another in the fear of Christ.

(Ephesians 5:19–21)

These characteristics are foreign to us because
they are not natural to our flesh. You know that
you are filled with the Spirit when you begin to
produce his fruit:

love, joy, peace, patience, kindness,
goodness, faithfulness, gentleness,
self-control.

(Galatians 5:22–23)

Overcoming the Devil by Putting On the Armor of God

As we have seen, overeating is a powerful tool used
by Satan to destroy you and to steal God's glory
in your life. You are most vulnerable to the devil's
attacks when you are caught up in the affairs
of everyday life and neglect God and his Word.

Satan has declared war on you, and you must fight according to God's military strategy. The idea that you are engaged in warfare can be frightening. Remember, this is spiritual warfare. You don't use human weapons, but the more powerful spiritual weapons found in God's Word.

Ephesians 6:10–18 lists all the weapons you need to defeat the devil. They are the belt of truth, the breastplate of righteousness, the shoes of the gospel of peace, the shield of faith, the helmet of salvation, and the sword of the Spirit. These weapons, powered by the Holy Spirit, are incredibly effective for destroying life-dominating sins. You must be ready, prepared and committed in your mind to fight in this war. Putting on the whole armor of God will enable you to overcome the sin of overeating. You must put on every piece of the armor of God. Not one part is to be neglected, or the devil will gain entry into your life.

The devil has already been defeated by Jesus Christ on the cross. You already have the victory. You need to live out that victory by putting on the whole armor of God.

CONCLUSION

First Corinthians 10:31 teaches us to glorify God in everything we do, whether eating, drinking, or doing any other mundane thing. In order to fulfill and live this out, you must commit your life to glorifying God when you eat. God's glory is to be your life's commitment. A wholehearted commitment to living a holy life, even when you eat, will help you overcome the influences and temptations of the world, the flesh, and the devil. The sin of overeating turns your focus away from God and toward your body, but, as you seek to honor God in your eating habits, overeating will no longer deceive you. You will never again believe the empty promise that indulging in food will satisfy your desires.

You honor God when you first confess your sin and receive his forgiveness (1 John 1:9). Second, you must repent of practicing the sin of overeating. You have not truly repented if you are only sorry for the consequences of overeating. True repentance means turning your heart completely away from indulging your flesh with food, and making the commitment of a lifetime: to love God with all your heart, with all your soul, and with all your mind (Matthew 22:37). True repentance means properly enjoying God's gift of food and eating with godly motives instead of following a legalistic diet regimen with ungodly motives.

Finally, you need to have a thankful heart. Elyse Fitzpatrick says, "God's creation is to be used and enjoyed by His children, and when we receive it with thankful prayer and with minds that are informed by Scripture, He blesses it to us and nourishes us by it."[6] You can truly walk in thankfulness instead of greed even though you live in a fallen world. A genuinely thankful heart is evidence that you have overcome the sin of overeating.

Personal Application Projects

Commit to the following five-week spiritual plan
to enable you to submit your eating habits to
God. God has given us specific strategies in his
Word for overcoming life-dominating sins. You
will need your Bible and a notebook or journal to
carry out the following five projects, which will
each take seven days.

WEEK 1: LET'S START AT THE BEGINNING

What is your story? When did your bad eating
habits begin? Describe at least three situations
when your eating got out of control. What did you
do to try to change your behavior? Why did you
allow yourself to overeat? What events in your life
caused you to overeat? Describe your battle with
the sin of overeating in the past.

WEEK 2: SEVEN-DAY DAILY QUIET TIME

Set aside 15–30 minutes each day to prayerfully
read Romans 6, 7, and 8. Read each chapter twice
over six days. Write down your thoughts and
insights as they pertain to your eating habits.

On the seventh day, read all three chapters in one sitting. Write down any spiritual insights from the Lord and record how your heart is being transformed.

WEEK 3: SEVEN-DAY DISCOVERY PROCESS

In order to discover your sinful eating patterns, you need to keep a daily record of what you eat. Record all instances of sinful eating, using one page of your journal for each day. Look for patterns throughout the day. What are the internal/emotional triggers? What are the external/environmental triggers? What types of food do you gravitate toward? Make a note of the times of day, and whether you are alone or with particular people.

WEEK 4: SEVEN-DAY GOAL-SETTING

If you are a believer in Christ, you are on a spiritual journey. The destination is transformation into the image of Jesus Christ. Goal-setting means planning the details of the trip so that you reach your destination. In your journal, pray and write down your physical, spiritual, relational, financial, and intellectual/educational goals as they pertain to your eating habits. Ask the Lord which goal he wants you to pursue first. Write it down. Develop a daily plan to achieve that goal as the Lord leads you. Track your setbacks and progress.

WEEK 5: SEVEN-DAY SCRIPTURE STUDY

Each day during this final week, read one of the Bible passages or groups of passages listed below and answer the following questions: What does the passage say about eating? What attitudes of the heart are being conveyed? What other descriptions and characteristics are associated with eating? What is God's perspective on eating in this passage? In light of these Scriptures, what attitudes and habits does God want me to change?

- Numbers 11:4–6; 33–34; Psalm 78:18–20; 22–32
- Proverbs 23:1–3
- Philippians 3:19
- Deuteronomy 21:20–21
- Titus 1:12
- Luke 12:19–20
- Luke 12:45–46

Where Can I Get More Help?

BOOKS

Betea, Ann Thomas, *God's Answer to Overeating: A Study of Scriptural Attitudes* (Lynwood, WA: Aglow Publications, 1986)

Fitzpatrick, Elyse, *Uncommon Vessels: A Program for Developing Godly Eating Habits* (Stanley, NC: Timeless Texts, 1990)

Morrone, Lisa, *Overcoming Overeating: It's Not What You Eat, It's What's Eating You!* (Eugene, OR: Harvest House, 2009)

OTHER RESOURCES

Setting Captives Free runs "The Lord's Table," a free 60-day interactive course that will teach you to enjoy a new-found relationship with the Lord and freedom from bad eating habits. Visit: www.settingcaptivesfree.com

"First Place 4 Health" is a Christ-centered, balanced weight-loss and healthy-living program that has guided hundreds of thousands of people to a healthy lifestyle and a closer walk with the Lord. Visit: www.firstplace4health.com

END NOTES

1   Elyse Fitzpatrick, *Love to Eat, Hate to Eat* (Eugene, OR: Harvest House, 1999), 108.

2   Quoted in Mike Cleveland, *The Lord's Table: A Biblical Approach to Weight Loss* (Newburyport, MA: Focus, 2003), 3

3   From John C. Broger, *Self-Confrontation: A Manual for In-Depth Discipleship* (Nashville: Thomas Nelson, 1994), 356.

4   Merriam-Webster's Collegiate Dictionary, vol. 1 (11th edn.; Springfield, MA: Merriam-Webster, Inc., 2003).

5   C. F. Keil and F. Delitzsch, *Commentary on the Old Testament, vol. 9* (repr.; Peabody, MA: Hendrickson, 2002), 102.

6   Fitzpatrick, *Love to Eat, Hate to Eat*, 123.

BOOKS IN THE HELP! SERIES INCLUDE...

(More titles in preparation)